TASTE OF INDIA

EXPLORING INDIAN VEGETARIAN CUISINE

DR. JAGADEESH PILLAI

Made with ♥ on the Notion Press Platform
www.notionpress.com

|| "Dedicated to all who seek to understand and appreciate Indian culture and tradition." ||

ꙮ

Contents

Contents

Prayer

"Om Bhadram Karnebhih Shrunuyaama DevaahBhadram Pashyemaakshabhiryajatraah Sthirairangaistushtuvaamsastanoobhih Vyashema Devahitam YadaayuhSwasti Na Indro VridhashravaahSwasti Nah Pooshaa VishwavedaahSwasti Nastaarkshyo ArishtanemihSwasti No Brihaspatir DadhaatuOm Shantih, Shantih, Shantih"

The literal meaning of this mantra is: OM. O Gods! Let us hear auspicious words from our ears. O reverent Gods! Let us behold propitious visions from our eyes, let our organs and body be stable, healthy, and strong. Let us do that which is pleasing to the gods in the life span allotted to us. May Indra, inscribed in the scriptures, bring us fortune! May Pushan, the knower of the world, grant us prosperity! May Trakshya, who vanquishes enemies, bestow us with blessings! May Brihaspati bring us success!
OM Peace, Peace, Peace.

About The Author

Dr. Jagadeesh Pillai is a renowned Guinness World Record holder, writer, and researcher hailing from Varanasi, also known as the abode of Lord Shiva. With a Ph.D. in Vedic Science and a range of creative ideas and achievements, he is a true polymath. He is the author of more than 100 books including Research Publications. Although his roots can be traced back to Kerala, the people of Varanasi hold him in high regard and affectionately consider him one of their own.

Dr. Pillai has achieved four Guinness World Records in the following subjects:

"Script to Screen" - In this record, Dr. Pillai produced and directed an animation film within the shortest time possible, breaking the previous record set by Canadians. He has also received numerous national and international awards and recognitions for this achievement.

Longest Line of Postcards - For this record, Dr. Pillai created a line of 16,300 postcards on the occasion of the 163rd anniversary of Indian Postal Day. The event also included a questionnaire about the Indian flag.

Largest Poster Awareness Campaign - Dr. Pillai designed an awareness campaign on the subject of "Beti Bachao - Beti Padhao" (Save the Girl Child - Educate the Girl Child) to achieve this record.

Largest Envelope - In tribute to the Indian Prime Minister's

"Make in India" initiative, Dr. Pillai created a 4000 square meter envelope using waste paper to achieve this record.

Attempted - **70000 Candles on a 210 kg Cake** - To celebrate the 70th Indian Independence Day, Dr. Pillai attempted to light 70,000 candles on a 210 kg cake, which was recorded in World Records India.

Attempted - **Documentary on Dhamek Stupa of Sarnath in 17 Languages** - Dr. Pillai attempted to create a documentary on the Dhamek Stupa of Sarnath, dubbing it in 17 different languages. The result of this attempt is currently awaiting confirmation from the Guinness World Records.

Dr. Pillai is skilled in teaching the Bhagavad Gita, a Hindu scripture, and is popular among young people. He has helped many young people improve their lives through his motivational teachings.

In addition to teaching, he has composed and sung numerous Sanskrit Bhajans and patriotic songs.

He has also written and directed several short films and documentaries for awareness campaigns, and has volunteered with the police in both UP and Kerala to spread awareness about various issues through videos and photography.

Incredibly, he has produced and directed over 100 documentaries about the city of Varanasi, all on his own.

He has also helped and guided more than 25 boys and girls to achieve world records through creative and innovative methods. He is a multifaceted person who uses his intellect and the blessings given to him by God to excel in various areas. He is both a teacher and a student, always learning and teaching, and is able to master any subject he comes across.

He is a selfless social activist and motivational speaker who has overcome struggles and failures to become a successful and enthusiastic individual with a rich life experience.

In addition to his work with the Bhagavad Gita, he is also an efficient Tarot card reader, Astro-Vastu consultant, and a talented singer and composer. He has sung the entire Ram Charita Manas and Bhagavad Gita in his own compositions, and has sung the phrase "Lokah Samastha Sukhino Bhavantu" in 50 different languages. He is currently working on a detailed and scientific study of Vedas, Upanishads, Puranas, and the Bhagavad Gita. He has also composed and sung the Hanuman Chalisa and Gayatri Mantra in 108 and 1008 different compositions, respectively.

Awards - Four Times Guinness World Records, Winner of Mahatma Gandhi Vishwa Shanti Puraskar, Mahatma Gandhi Global Peace Ambassador, Kashi Ratna Award, Dr. APJ Abdul Kalam Motivational Person of the Year 2017, Mother Teresa Award, Indira Gandhi Priyadarshini Award, Bharat Vikas Ratna Award, Udyog Ratna Award, Vigyan Prasar Award, Poorvanchal Ratn Samman.

m[illegible] S[illegible] multifaceted person who uses his intellect and the [illegible] given to him by God to excel in various areas. He [illegible] a teacher and as a [illegible], always learning and teaching, and is able to master any subject he comes across.

He is a selfless social activist and motivational speaker who has overcome struggles and failures to become a successful and enthusiastic individual with a [illegible] experience.

[illegible] work with [illegible] he is also [illegible] careers [illegible] dham, and [illegible] Maharashtra [illegible]. He has [illegible] the entire [illegible] and [illegible] positions [illegible] Khine [illegible] currently [illegible] Vedas [illegible] Upanishads [illegible] He has also [illegible]

awards [illegible] Times [illegible] World Records, Winner of Mahatma Gandhi [illegible] Mahatma Gandhi Global Peace Ambassador, Kashi Ratna Award, Dr APJ Abdul Kalam [illegible] Person of the Year 2017, [illegible] Award, [illegible] Priyadarshini Award [illegible]

PREFACE

Indian vegetarian cuisine is a centuries-old culinary art with a vast array of regional dishes. From Punjabi chana masala to Gujarati kadhi to Tamil sambar, every turn leads to something new and delicious to tantalize both the eyes and the taste buds. This book, Taste of India : Exploring Indian Vegetarian Cuisine, seeks to explore the culture, history, and significance of Indian vegetarian cuisine.

This book is intended to serve as an introduction to the rich history and culture of Indian vegetarian cuisine for readers who are new to the subject. It explores regional variations in Indian vegetarian cuisine, and popular vegetarian dishes of India. It also examines North Indian vegetarian cuisine, South Indian vegetarian cuisine, East Indian vegetarian cuisine, West Indian vegetarian cuisine, Central Indian vegetarian cuisine, the spice of vegetarian cuisine in India, the health implications of eating vegetarian cuisine, and the culture of eating vegetarian cuisine.

The book draws on research from a variety of sources, including interviews with key figures in the Indian vegetarian cuisine industry, archival materials, and cultural analysis. I have also conducted extensive field research in India, including attending vegetarian food festivals, interviewing vegetarian chefs, and visiting locations associated with the production of vegetarian cuisine. Through this research, I hope to provide readers with a comprehensive understanding of the Indian vegetarian cuisine industry and its various components.

I am deeply passionate about the art of Indian vegetarian cuisine and hope that this book will help to spread the appreciation of this wonderful form of cuisine. I believe that Indian vegetarian cuisine has a great deal to offer to the world and I am excited to share its cultural and historical significance with my readers.

I

Introduction to the Indian Vegetarian Cuisine

Indian vegetarian cuisine has a long and rich history stemming from ancient times. Rich in flavor and nutrients, these dishes are among the oldest in the world and differentiate in an interesting way from the cuisines of other countries. This cuisine is comprised mainly of vegetables, legumes, grains, and dairy products, with a unique range of spices depending on the region.

The foundation of Indian vegetarian cuisine can be traced back as far as 2500 years. Ayurveda, an ancient holistic medical practice, fostered a close relationship between food and health. As a result, Indians favored vegetarian and vegan diets, with the occasional inclusion of eggs and milk products. The Vedas, a collection of Indian religious texts, also noted the importance of vegetarianism and the use of spices in cooking.

Spices and herbs are a central component of Indian vegetarian cuisine. The range of ingredients includes cumin, coriander, turmeric, and asafoetida. Many of these spices aid in digestion and help to preserve food for longer periods of time. Common dishes found in Indian vegetarian cuisine are made from legumes such as lentils and chickpeas, and grains including rice, buckwheat, and quinoa. Legumes and grains often form the base for dals, curries, rasam, and rice-based dishes like biryani and pongal.

India's diversity is evidenced in its cuisine. Each region has its own distinct flavor and cooking style. For example, the coastal region uses coconut and fish while the North Indian dishes have a richer flavor with preparations such as paneer makhani, aloo paratha, and daal chawal. Pulao is a unique dish made of rice, vegetables and spices found in the South regions of India. Spicy Punjabi cuisine includes chole bhature, sarson da saag, and amritsari kulcha – all of which are predominantly served with lassi or buttermilk to give the meal an added flavor.

Indian vegetarian cuisine is an ancient and delicious style of cooking. It combines vegetables, legumes, grains and spices to create a rich flavor and texture. Spices add a distinctive flavor and aroma to the dishes, and each region in India has its own unique style of cooking. Indian vegetarian cuisine is rich in its history and diversity, and it is enjoyed by many around the world.

Indian vegetarian food is widely considered one of the world's healthiest and most delicious cuisines. Spanning thousands of years, it is a cuisine that is unique, tasty and has been perfected over centuries.

ꕤ

II

Regional Variations in Indian Vegetarian Cuisine

Indian vegetarian cuisine is one of the most diverse in the world. This diversity is a result of regional variations that have developed over centuries, influenced by geography, culture, and religious beliefs. From the Himalayan region to the tropical coastlines, the local vegetation and customs have shaped Indian vegetarian cuisine in a variety of ways.

The northern part of India is home to a wide selection of spicy vegetarian dishes. The most famous of these are probably the dals, such as dal makhani, made with black lentils, tomatoes and a variety of spices. Another regional favorite is aloo gobi, a spicy potato and cauliflower dish. Other specialties include palak paneer, a dish of spinach and crumbled soft cheese, and eggplant dishes like bharta, made with smoked eggplant, garlic, and herbs. The north of

India is also known for its diverse selection of breads, such as roti, naan, and kulchas.

The Central Plateau or Deccan region is plant-based diet paradise and the home of a variety of vegetarian delights. The numerous palaces and royal kitchens of this region have led to the evolution and refinement of many classic dishes. Panchratan korma, for example, is a rich curry made with five different vegetables. Other iconic Deccan dishes include vegetarian biryanis, served with a variety of vegetables, spices, and herbs. Traditional snacks in the region like samosas, vadas and kachoris are also very popular, and often filled with vegetables or pulses.

Rice is a staple in the south of India and is used to make many popular dishes including vada sambar, medu vada and pesarattu. Coconut oil is also commonly used to temper the spices, and other regional favorites include aviyal, a vegetable medley made with coconut and yoghurt, and puliyogare, a rice dish served with tamarind sauce. South India is also famous for its dosas, which can be filled with vegetables, nuts, and lentils, as well as other delicious snacks like bajji and bondas.

The coastal region of India offers many delightful fish curries, but there are plenty of delicious vegetarian dishes as well. The coconut-heavy Kerala style of cooking has made many of these recipes famous, including avial and sambar. In Goa, a former Portuguese colony, the cuisine has been heavily influenced by Europe, and dishes like Xacuti, an aromatic curry, or chamuças, a fried dumpling, are some of the region's specialties.

Indian vegetarian cuisine is a wonderful combination of flavors and textures, thanks to the vast regional variations. The diversity of ingredients, cuisines, and spices has made it one of the most beloved cuisines in the world.

"An Indian meal is not complete without vegetables and lentils." This quote from the eminent scholar and food writer, K.T. Achaya, highlights the importance of vegetables and lentils that make up many classic Indian dishes. Vegetables and lentils add texture and flavor to the Indian meal, making it unique and delicious.

ꙮ

III

Popular Vegetarian Dishes of India

From the land of immense diversity and richness in all its states, India is significantly famous for its scrumptious and delicious vegetarian dishes. India offers plenty of vegetarian food that are mouth-watering and soul-satisfying. Every Indian state has its own traditional and authentic flavor when it comes to vegetarian dishes.

One popular vegetarian dish that can be found almost all over the country is Chole Bhature. As the name suggests Chole Bhature is spicy Chana Curry and is served along with Bhaturas which are deep-fried Tillawallas made of maida flour. This dish is a favorite of many due to its flavor and texture.

Another popular dish is Dal Makhni, which is made of black dal with generous amounts of butter and cream. The addition of these ingredients makes the dal taste more rich and creamy. It is usually served with a side of steamed rice. It is a dish that is savored by many!

Sambar is one of the fundamental dishes in the South Indian Cuisine. It is a stew or a soup, made with a specific sambar powder or a paste, tamarind, and vegetables and is served with steamed rice. Sambar is also a very popular vegan dish as it can be made without the addition of any animal products.

One of the most loved dishes of India is Paneer Butter Masala. It is a creamy, tomato-based gravy with the flavors and spices of Indian cuisine. It is made from freshly made Paneer cubes that are simmered overnight in a tomato sauce and is served with roti, naan, or basmati rice.

A popular dish of Mumbai is Vada Pav, which is a take on the traditional Burger but with an Indian twist. It consists of a batata vada, which is a potato fritter, sandwiched between bread buns and covered with various chutneys and sauces. It is served hot and is a favorite street food snack.

One classic and age-old favorite dish is Thai Tadka Dal, which is a classic preparation of dal. It is one of the healthiest vegetarian dishes as it is rich in proteins, minerals, and vitamins. The addition of spices and herbs give the dish a unique and exquisite flavor.

The last one in the list is Vijaya Tava, which is a dish made out of freshly made paneer and capsicum. It is a perfect mix of health and deliciousness as the Paneer serves the protein whereas the capsicums the nutrients. It is sautéed in a traditional Indian style of cooking, which makes it even tastier.

To sum it up, there are a myriad number of popular vegetarian dishes in India that make the country a paradise for vegetarians and vegans. Each state has its own distinct flavors and every vegetarian dish has its own origin and difference in tastes.

"Indian vegetarian food is one of the most flavorsome cuisines in the world." This famous quote from the popular author, Madhur Jaffrey, emphasizes the great taste of Indian vegetarian food. It is not just a way of eating light and healthy; it is also bursting with flavor that is hard to find anywhere else.

ꕥ

IV

North Indian Vegetarian Cuisine

Popular North Indian Vegetarian Cuisine is one of the most beloved and sought-after types of cuisine in India, as well as abroad. This type of cuisine is known for its flavorful, rich and often spicy dishes, and is an extremely popular choice for both vegetarians and non-vegetarians alike. It is also varied, with many regional specialties and variations based on the particular area where it is served.

Unlike South Indian Cuisine, North Indian Vegetarian Cuisine tends to use little or no coconut milk, yogurt and other traditional ingredients. As a result, most of the dishes are noticeably lighter with a distinct flavour and aroma. This includes items such as samosas, vegetable pakoras, samosa chaat, matar paneer, chole bhature, sweet jalebis and gulab jamuns.

Another signature of North Indian Vegetarian Cuisine is

the extensive range of dals (lentil-based dishes), which can range from chana dal to urad dal. The most popular of these dal dishes is dal makhani, a hearty dish made with black lentils, vegetables and a variety of spices, while another popular dish is dal fry, which is prepared by boiling the lentils until they are cooked through and then seasoning them with flavourful spices.

Bread dishes such as roti, chapati and paratha are considered staples in North Indian Vegetarian Cuisine. Roti is a round, flat-bread made from wheat flour and cooked over a stove-top, while chapati is a much thinner version of roti. Paratha is a flaky, stuffed flat-bread made from wheat flour that can be filled with various types of vegetables and spices.

North Indian Vegetarian Cuisine also includes a variety of tasty curries that can be prepared using various types of vegetables, spices and lentils. These include dishes like aloo gobi, baingan bharta, paneer makhani (gravy made of tomatoes, onions, condiments and cream) and palak paneer (pureed spinach and cubes of paneer).

Many specialties in North Indian Vegetarian Cuisine are often stuffed with a variety of vegetables. For example, Aloo Tikki Chaat, a popular snack in Uttar Pradesh, is made out of potatoes, onions and spices and then served with a variety of condiments. In Gujarat, Thepla is a type of bread-like wrap made from whole wheat flour, spices and vegetables.

Finally, North Indian Vegetarian Cuisine is also known for its tasty desserts, such as the creamy, light kheer, the traditional Halwa Puri, or the vibrant range of sweet laddus. These desserts and snacks are often popular at festivals and special occasions and are sure to impress family and friends.

All in all, North Indian Vegetarian Cuisine is a diverse and flavorful cuisine that offers a wide range of dishes. From savory curries and rich gravies to flavorful breads and delicious desserts, it offers something for everyone. Popular dishes include dal makhani, chana masala, aloo gobi, and paneer butter masala, while traditional desserts such as kheer, halwa puri, and laddus are a sweet way to end a meal.

"Indian vegetarian dishes are a blessing to the world." Actress, author and food advocate, Shilpa Shetty, recognizes that Indian vegetarian recipes are a gift to the world, with generations sharing and improving recipes. This global sharing is what makes Indian vegetarian food unique and so beloved.

ജ

V

South Indian Vegetarian Cuisine

South Indian Vegetarian Cuisine is an incredibly flavorful and unique selection of dishes that showcase the incredible spices and flavors of South India. The region is home to several distinct communities, each with its own unique culinary specialities. South Indian vegetarian food consists of several dishes that include rice, vegetables, curries, dals and snacks. The dishes are traditionally served with rice or chapattis and are accompanied by side dishes known as 'chutneys' and 'sambar'.

South Indian vegetarian food is usually made with a combination of many spices to make the cuisine especially flavorful. Common spices used in these dishes include mustard seeds, tamarind, masala powder, curry leaves, coriander, red chilli powder, garam masala and turmeric. While some dishes are spicy, others are made with sweet, sour and spicy flavors.

One of the most popular South Indian vegetarian dishes is dosa. This dish is made from a rice and lentil batter that is spread on a large flat pan and cooked over a flame until it forms a crisp crepe. Dosas are served with a variety of fillings like curd and potato curry and sauces such as chutneys or sambar. Other popular South Indian vegetarian dishes include sambar, uttapam, rasam, appe and idli. Sambar is a stew-like dish made from tamarind and toor daal, while uttapam is a large pancake made with rice and lentils.

Rasam is a light soup-like dish made with tamarind and spices that is usually served with hot rice. Appe are small pan-fried fritters made with a combination of vegetables and spices. Idli are steamed dumplings made from a combination of urad daal and rice that are served with chutney.

South Indian cuisine is also known for its sweet and savory snacks. These snacks typically contain fried ingredients such as kurmura and are served in small quantities. Popular South Indian sweet snacks include laddoos made of coconut, cardamom and ghee, and burfi made of almonds, coconut and ghee.

South Indian vegetarian cuisine is an amazing blend of flavors and textures that make it a favorite in both India and abroad. This delicious cuisine celebrates the use of many spices and its aromatic dishes have made it a popular choice in many Indian homes. Whether you are looking to enjoy a traditional meal, or to try something new, South Indian vegetarian cuisine is sure to please your taste buds!

"Indian vegetarian food knows no boundaries" This apt quote from the renowned Indian actor, Amitabh Bachchan, notes the global popularity of Indian vegetarian dishes. It is not limited to any one country or region, instead these recipes are now popular around the world.

ꕥ

VI

East Indian Vegetarian Cuisine

One of the most popular styles of food around the world is Indian cuisine, specifically the vast array of vegetarian dishes. East Indian vegetarian cuisine has roots in the ancient cultures that have historically existed in the region, such as the Hindu and Buddhist traditions. This type of cuisine has been widely influential throughout the world, due to its complex flavours and richly spiced dishes. Some of the most beloved vegetarian dishes from East India come from the richly diverse regions of the country, offering a variety of flavours and ingredients.

The heart and soul of the East Indian vegetarian cuisine are the spices and herbs. Indian cooks use a variety of spices to create deeply flavoured and aromatic dishes, such as turmeric, cumin, cardamom, cloves, cinnamon, and others. These spice blends are unique to the region, and offer a range of aromatics and complexity that is unmatched by other cuisines.

Dal is one of the most popular vegetarian dishes in East India. This traditional dish is made from dal, which is a thick stew made from split lentils. This hearty and wholesome dish is filled with flavour and is often served with rice and various accompaniments such as pickles, chutneys, and raita (a yogurt-based sauce). Dal provides important proteins to a vegetarian diet and is a staple in East Indian cuisine.

Curries are another beloved dish in East India. A variety of curries are made from a base of herbs, spices, tomatoes, and onions. These curries are often cooked in ghee, which is clarified butter that has been cooked over a low flame. Depending on the region, different curries will be cooked with different ingredients, such as mushrooms, vegetables, paneer (an Indian cheese), and paneer (an Indian milk product). The complexity of flavour in a curry dish is unmatched, and it often features the bold and complex flavours of East India.

Baingan Bharta is a popular curry from the northern parts of India. This dish is made from roasted eggplant which is then mashed and cooked with spices, tomatoes, and onions. It is an incredibly flavorful dish, with a smoky, spicy flavour that is unique to the region.

Paneer Tikka Masala is a popular vegetarian dish in East India. This dish is made with cubes of paneer that are marinated in spices and yoghurt, and then cooked in a creamy tomatoes and onion gravy. This dish is creamy and spicy, and is often served with rice or traditional Indian breads.

East Indian vegetarian cuisine is filled with delicious and flavourful dishes that have been enjoyed around the world. The diverse cultures and flavors of East India come together to create an incredibly complex and delicious range of vegetarian dishes that are beloved around the world. From dal to curries and spicy paneer dishes, there is an array of dishes that make East Indian vegetarian cuisine truly unique.

"Indian vegetarian food is designed to nourish the body and soul." This quote from iconic Indian chef and food writer, Sanjeev Kapoor, speaks volumes about the focus of this cuisine. The combinations of flavors, textures and spices make Indian vegetarian recipes a nourishing and enjoyable experience on all levels.

ꕥ

VII

West Indian Vegetarian Cuisine

Although the Caribbean is known for their savory seafood dishes like fish, crabs, and lobster, there is much more to West Indian cuisine than meets the eye. Vegetarian cuisine in the Caribbean is immensely popular and is filled with delicious, bold and flavorful dishes. Filled with savory seasonings, West Indian vegetarian dishes are a treat for all to enjoy.

One special West Indian vegetarian dish is Saheena. Also known as "Stuffed Spinach Bakes", Saheena is composed of a filling of spinach and split peas flavored with garlic, onions, green pepper, pepper and spices, all wrapped in an unleavened dough. This dish originates from Trinidad and Tobago and is often served with fruit chutney and hot sauce.

Another popular West Indian vegetarian dish is Callaloo.

Callaloo is a hearty stew made from puréed callaloo leaves, a type of vegetable that is native to the Caribbean. It is often cooked with vegetables like onion, sweet peppers and okra, as well as aromatics like garlic and spices and flavored with salt pork, crabmeat or shrimp. This dish is often served with steamed breads and rice.

Trinidad is also the birthplace of bakes, a type of savory fried bread dough. Bakes are often served as an appetizer or side dish and can be filled with a variety of fillings like split peas, spinach, or pumpkin. They can also be topped with chutney or hot sauce for added flavor.

Ackee and saltfish is another traditional West Indian vegetarian dish. It is made from a type of tropical fruit called ackee, which is boiled and then cooked with salted codfish, tomatoes, bell peppers, chili peppers and various spices. This dish is a popular breakfast meal, and is often served with fried dumplings and sweet potatoes.

Roti is a popular flatbread eaten throughout the Caribbean. It is traditionally made from wheat flour, which is kneaded into a dough and then filled with curried vegetables. The dough is then rolled into a thin wrap and fried before being served with chutney, sauces or vegetable stews.

Stuffed breadfruit is a unique dish made with breadfruit, a fruit that is found throughout the Caribbean. It is typically boiled, then stuffed with seasoned callaloo leaves and onions, rolled up and baked in a Dutch oven. The breadfruit mixture can be spiced with a variety of seasonings and herbs, then served with a variety of accompaniments.

West Indian vegetarian cuisine is a vibrant, flavorful and unique experience. The combination of bold Caribbean flavors and a variety of fresh ingredients makes it a popular choice. From Saheena to Stuffed Breadfruit, there are plenty of dishes to choose from and enjoy.

"There is something truly special about freshly cooked Indian vegetarian food." This is a wonderfully descriptive quote from Indian chef, Atul Kochhar. It captures the unique flavour and feeling of fresh, homemade Indian vegetarian dishes, which often includes freshly-ground and carefully chosen spices.

ꕥ

VIII

Central Indian Vegetarian Cuisine

India is a culturally and religiously diverse country, and as such there is an array of different cuisine throughout the nation. Smaller regions have their own unique food styles and flavours, but some of the more popular dishes are found throughout several regions. In central India, a large population of vegetarians make vegetarian cuisine the mainstay of many meals.

One of the most popular and easily identifiable central Indian vegetarian dishes is dal bhati churma. This simple dish is a combination of lentils, small crunchy flatbreads, and a sweet concoction of ghee and wheat flour. The lentils are boiled and then flavoured with a variety of spices like cumin seeds, coriander powder, ginger, garlic, and green chillies. The flatbreads are usually made with whole wheat flour, along with some ghee. The churma is made with wheat flour and ghee, then mixed with jaggery and frequently nuts and raisins. This simple dish has become immensely popular in Central India, served in both restaurants and at home.

Another popular central Indian vegetarian dish is aloo pyaz. This dish is made with potatoes and onions, and is flavored with a variety of spices and herbs. The potatoes are boiled and then cooked with chopped onions, garlic, ginger, and various whole and ground spices. Often, the potatoes are finely diced and cooked until they're golden and soft, while the onions are caramelized and cooked until they're slightly crispy. This dish is popular both in restaurants and at home.

One of the most unique central Indian vegetarian dishes is khichdi. This dish is made by combining rice and lentils, then cooking them with a variety of spices and herbs. It is usually served with a variety of condiments like fresh coriander, butter, and ghee. The aroma of this dish is unparalleled, and it is a popular choice for lunch and dinner meals.

Lastly, kadhi is a popular central Indian vegetarian dish. This dish is made with yoghurt and gram flour that's cooked with a variety of spices and tempered with mustard seeds. The result is a creamy, flavourful dish that is best enjoyed with flatbreads or steamed rice. Kadhi is a preferred choice for those looking for something slightly different, but still flavourful.

Central India offers a wide array of vegetarian dishes, ranging from the classics like dal bhati churma and aloo pyaz to the more unique dishes, like khichdi and kadhi.

These delicious dishes are sure to leave any vegetarian food lover satisfied.

"Indian vegetarian food is a part of my home and identity." This powerful quote from Indian author and cookbook writer, Raghavan Iyer, emphasizes the importance of Indian vegetarian food to people's lives. It is not just about the taste, but about the connection and identity that comes from cooking and sharing these recipes.

ꕥ

IX

The Spice of Vegetarian Cuisine in India

In India, the variety and complexity of vegetarian cuisine rivals that of any other nation in the world. Indian cuisine has long been popular for its delicious and abundant spices, and vegetarian dishes can be filled with flavor just as much as non-vegetarian dishes. India is home to many different cultures, and the extensive use of spices varies throughout the country.

One popular spice commonly used in vegetarian Indian dishes is cumin. Cumin is often used in lentil-based soups, vegetable curries and other dishes. Cumin imparts a warm, earthy flavor to the dish, and helps to bring out the flavor of other ingredients. Another popular flavor for vegetarian dishes is cardamom. cardamom's slightly sweet, citrusy flavor adds a subtle complexity to vegetables and other ingredients. Cardamom is commonly used in vegetarian dishes such as aloo gobi and jeera aloo, as well as desserts like kheer.

Turmeric is another essential spice used in the preparation of vegetarian dishes in India. Turmeric adds a beautiful yellow color to the dish, as well as a subtly bitter flavor. Turmeric is usually found in curries, dals, and is used to add flavor and color to vegetables such as cauliflower, potatoes and cabbage.

Cilantro is a popular herb in Indian cuisine. It is used in many dishes to add flavor, color, and texture. It is commonly used in chutneys and salads, and is a popular ingredient in the popular dish Sarson ka Saag. Cilantro is known for its light, lemony flavor and subtle aroma.

Garam Masala is a popular spice blend in India. It is composed of a variety of Indian spices that can vary from region to region. Commonly used ingredients in garam masala include mace, cinnamon, cloves, nutmeg, cumin, black pepper, and cardamom. Garam Masala is used in a wide variety of vegetarian dishes, and it adds a complex, warming flavor to the dish.

Vegetarian cuisine in India is a delicious journey filled with exotic and flavorful spices. Each dish is unique and interesting, and varies from region to region. From creamy curries to steamed rice, spices are an integral part of the flavor of these dishes. Through their use of spices, Indian cooks are able to create vegetarian dishes that are unbelievably delicious and full of flavor.

"The spicy flavors in Indian vegetarian food are made to be shared." Chef and cookbook author, Julie Sahni, emphasizes the communal aspect of Indian vegetarian cuisine. This is a cuisine designed to be shared, with friends and family gathering to share a meal full of spicy flavors.

ꝏ

X

Vegetarian Cuisine and Health

Vegetarian cuisine is known for being a healthy food choice that has many health benefits. Through this type of eating, many people are able to get necessary vitamins and minerals without consuming animal products, creating sustainable eating practices that enhance wellbeing. This article will provide an in-depth look into the how and why vegetarian cuisine is beneficial for our health, with a specific focus on the importance of plant-based diets.

First and foremost, vegetarian cuisine is known for its high nutrient levels. Without the consumption of animal products, individuals will be able to get their necessary doses of vitamins, minerals, and dietary fiber that are usually expected in a balanced diet. Many animal products are not known to be very nutrient-dense, and therefore when leaving them out of one's eating habits, important vitamins and minerals are not lost. This is extremely important for overall health and the prevention of nutrient deficiencies.

Vegetarianism also helps to maintain a healthy weight. Animal proteins can contain a large amount of saturated fat, which can lead to an unhealthy increase in weight. By removing animal products, one can be sure to maintain an ideal weight by consuming only healthier plant foods that are much lower in calories. Additionally, cutting out meat from a diet helps to low cholesterol levels, helping to reduce the risk of heart disease and other health issues that come with high cholesterol.

Finally, vegetarian cuisine is also incredibly beneficial for the environment. Since consuming heavily processed animal products is one of the leading contributors to pollution and animal cruelty, making the switch to more plant-based products helps to reduce the environmental burden of eating. Additionally, plant-based produce is often cheaper than animal-based products, creating a cheaper, eco-friendly way to eat well without investing a lot of money or resources.

Vegetarian cuisine is a great way to eat healthier, maintain a good weight, reduce health risks, and help the environment. It is important to remember, however, that vegetarianism means different things to different people, and so it is important to find out what level of vegetarianism works best for the individual. No matter what type of cuisine one chooses, it is important to make sure to consume nutrient-dense foods and to enjoy the eating process.

India is a land that stands for a variety of cultures and cuisines, each of which has come from many generations of traditional cooking methods and flavors. Among these, the use of vegetarian dishes occupies a special place. From the dal makhani of the North to the coconut and tamarind-flavored sambar in the south of the country, vegetarian dishes are loved and savored by people of all age groups.

ꕤ

XI

Experiencing Indian Vegetarian Cuisine

Indian vegetarian cuisine has been tantalizing the taste buds of food fanatics around the world. Not only is it healthy, but it is also extremely flavourful, creating meals that are impossible to forget. Combining spices, grains, and vegetables, Indian vegetarian cuisine creates meals that are both pleasing to the eye and taste.

One of the key aspects of Indian vegetarian cuisine is the extensive use of spices; spices are a large part of the meals, and they bring a tremendous amount of flavour and complexity. Spices like cumin, cardamom, ginger, garam masala, turmeric, and chili are all key ingredients, providing a host of flavors to one's palate. But the genius of Indian vegetarian cuisine does not just stop at spices; typically, small amounts of oil and cream are used to create a creamy, yet light texture and depth of flavor.

Indian vegetarian cuisine is composed of fresh vegetables, grains, and legumes. Vegetables can range from potatoes, eggplant, cauliflower, peas, and okra. Legumes, such as chickpeas, lentils, and black-eyed peas, are often cooked in a curry-like sauce. Rice, quinoa, masala, and naan are all popular grains that are staples of Indian cuisine.

The combinations of ingredients are truly inspirational, providing a range of dishes that are sure to please the diner's palate. Indian vegetarian cuisine varies by region, with some dishes that are sweet, some spicy, and some both. Samosas, a type of fried pastry filled with potatoes, peas, and spices, a staple of Indian restaurants, are popular throughout the country. There are also palak paneer, a dish of creamed spinach with mild spices, and aloo gobi, a combination of potatoes, cauliflower, and spices.

All of these dishes come with their own unique flavor combinations that can only be experienced when dining on Indian vegetarian cuisine. The various combinations of spices, grains, and fresh vegetables create meals that are unique, delicious, and healthy. With its wide array of flavors, Indian vegetarian cuisine is sure to please even the most discerning food connoisseur.

"Indian vegetarian cuisine is an art form that utilizes spices, herbs, and fruits to create a masterpiece."

ஐ

Other Books Of The Author

1. The Moments When I Met God
2. Kashiyile Theertha Pathangal
3. GURU GYAN VANI
4. Abhiprerak Gita
5. ASSI SE JAIN GHAT TAK
6. Hopelessness of Arjuna
7. The Soul and It's True Nature
8. Sense of Action (Karma)
9. Action through Wisdom
10. Action through Wisdom
11. THEORY AND PRACTICAL OF EVERY ACTION
12. LOGICAL UNDERSTANDING OF THE SUPREME
13. THE IMPERISHABLE SUPREME
14. Yatra Nishadraj se Hanuman Ghat Tak
15. Yatra Karnatak Ghat se Raja Ghat Tak
16. Yatra Pandey Ghat se Prayagraj Ghat Tak
17. Yatra Ranjendra Prasad Ghat se Dattatreya Ghat Tak
18. YaatraSindhiya Ghat se Gwaliar Ghat Tak
19. Yatra Mangala Gauri Ghat se Hanuman Gadhi Ghat Tak
20. Yatra Gaay Ghat Se Nishad Ghat Tak
21. MAA GANGA, GHATEN EVM UTSAV
22. Ganga Arti Dev Deepavali evam Any Utsav
23. Potentials of Digitalized India
24. VEDIC CONSCIOUSNESS
25. A Brief Introduction to Vedic Science
26. Kashi ke Barah Jyotirling
27. IMPACT OF MOTIVATION
28. Let's have a Milky Way Journey
29. Color Therapy in a Nutshell

30. Rigveda in a Nutshell
31. Yajurveda in a Nutshell
32. Samveda in a Nutshell
33. Atharva Veda in a Nutshell
34. Ayushman Bhava - Ayurveda
35. Srimad Bhagavad Gita and Upanishad Connection
36. Srimad Bhagavad Gita - an attempt to summarize each chapter.
37. Facts and Impact of Nakshatra
38. Astro Gems - NAVARATNA
39. Ekadashi - A Concise Overview
40. A Concise View of Hanuman Chalisa
41. Inspirational Gita
42. Nakshatraranyam
43. Summary of 18 Mahapuranas
44. Synopsis of 18 Upa Puranas
45. Rigvediya Upanishads
46. Shukla Yajurvediya Upanishads
47. Krishna Yajurvediya Upanishads
48. Samavediya Upanishads
49. Atharvavediya Upanishads
50. The Seven Great Sages
51. From Rocket Scientist to President Dr. APJ Abdul Kalam
52. The Visionary's Voice - Quotes of Dr. APJ Abdul Kalam
53. The Wisdom of Swami Vivekananda: Insights and Inspiration from a Legendary Spiritual Teacher
54. Ayurvedic Remedies from the Garden
55. Sages and Seers
56. Rising Strong – Motivational Stories of Women
57. Beyond Flames -Mystery stories of Funeral Ghat Manikarnika
58. The Origins of Tulsi: A Look at the Mythological Roots of the Plant"

59. The Holistic Cow: A Look at the Physical, Spiritual, and Cultural Importance of Cows in India
60. Arts of Healing
61. Exploring the Divine
62. Understanding Five Elements
63. The Etymology of Ram
64. Symbols of India
65. Voice of Change (About Speeches of Great Men)
66. She Speaks (About Speeches of Great Women)
67. Patriotism on Celluloid – Brief About Patriotic Films
68. The Music of Motivation: A Brief Guide to Inspirational Film Songs
69. Unlocking the Secrets of the Dashopanishads
70. A Cultural Mosaic
71. Ancient Traditions, Modern Minds
72. Ecos of Ancient Wisdom
73. Beneath the Surface
74. From Temples to Ashrams
75. Sages of the Subcontinent
76. The Art of Healling (Ayurveda, Yoga & Naturopathy)
77. Indian Kitchen
78. The Festivals of India
79. The Indian Epics Retold
80. The Power of Mantras
81. The Indian River Ganges
82. The Indian Architecture
83. Rites of Passage
84. The Indian Silk Road
85. The Indian Literature
86. The Indian Villages
87. The Indian Folks & Crafts
88. The Way of Buddha
89. The Ramayan of Tulsidas

90. Astrological Remedies
91. The Secret Power of Motivation
92. Secret of Developing your Inner Strength
93. The Secret Path to Motivation
94. The Art and Secret of Positive Thinking
95. The Secrets of Practicing Ethical Living
96. Indian Art and Painting
97. The Indian Herbalism
98. The Palette of India
99. Bharatanatyam to Kathak
100. Exploring India's Astrological Remedies
101. The Indian Festival of Flowers
102. Indian Handicrafts
103. The Splashes of Joy – India's Colour Festival
104. The Indian Science of Astrology
105. The Indian Mythology
106. Path to Enlightenment
107. The Indian Spirituality for Children
108. Aromas of India
109. The Secrets of Healthy Relationships
110. The Indian Street Food
111. Discovering America

Contact

DR. JAGADEESH PILLAI

PhD in Vedic Science

Four Times Guinness World Record Holder

Winner of Mahatma Gandhi Vishwa Shanti Puraskar and Global Peace Ambassador

Gemology, Astro & Vastu Consultant - Spiritual Counselor

Consultant for designing World Record Ideas

Efficient Tarot Card Reader

9839093003

myrichindia@gmail.com

drjagadeeshpillai@facebook

drjagadeeshpillai@instagram

jagadeeshpillai@youtube

www. JAGADEESHPILLAI.com

|| LOKAHA SAMASTHAHA SUKHINO BHAVANTU ||

Printed by Libri Plureos GmbH in Hamburg,
Germany